Let's eat Breakfast

Clare Hibbert

First published in paperback 2011,
by Evans Brothers Limited
2A Portman Mansions
Chiltern Street
London W1U 6NR

Produced for Evans Brothers Limited by
White-Thomson Publishing Ltd

Printed by Everbest in China
July 2011, job number (CAG1678)

Educational consultant: Sue Palmer MEd FRSA FEA
Project manager: Clare Hibbert
Picture research: Amy Sparks
Design: Balley Design Limited
Creative director: Simon Balley
Designer/Illustrator: Michelle Tilly

British Library Cataloguing in Publication Data

Hibbert, Clare 1970–
        Let's eat breakfast. - (Sparklers) 1. Breakfasts - Pictorial works -
        Juvenile literature 2. Food habits - Pictorial works - Juvenile literature
        I. Title
        394.1'5

ISBN: 978 0 2375 3417 2

Contents

Breakfast time......................4

Hot toast...........................6

Cereals............................ 8

Pick and mix.......................10

Something to drink..............12

Breakfast eggs....................14

All kinds of breads...............16

Rice and fish.......................18

Make it: Muesli.................. 20

Notes for adults..................22

Index...............................24

Breakfast time

ring

ring

ring

This book is about breakfast.

Hot toast

pop!

Some people eat toast for breakfast.

What do **you** have with **your toast?**

7

Cereals

Porridge is a breakfast cereal made from oats.

brrm

brrm

combine harvester →

This farmer is harvesting oats.

9

Pick and mix

Breakfast can be slices of cooked meats and cheese...

...or juicy fruit.

11

Something to drink

Which breakfast drinks are hot?

Milk for drinks can come from cows, sheep or goats.

13

Breakfast Eggs

Eggs can be scrambled...

All kinds of breads

chapati

Breads and pastries make a filling breakfast.

brush

This baker is making croissants (say 'kwa- son').

17

Rice and fish

Congee (say 'kon-zhay') is rice porridge.

Breakfast in Japan

This breakfast has tasty fish.

Make it: Muesli

Mix these things together to make muesli.

- oats ✓
- raisins ✓
- apple juice ✓
- grated apple ✓
- hazelnuts* ✓

* Miss these out if you have a nut allergy.

It tastes delicious with plain yogurt and honey.

21

Notes for adults

Sparklers books are designed to support and extend the learning of young children. The **Food We Eat** titles won a Practical Pre-School Sliver Award, the **Body Moves** titles won a Practical Pre-School Gold Award and the **Out and About** titles won the 2009 Practical Pre-School Gold Overall Winner Award. The books' high-interest subjects link in to the Early Years Foundation Stage curriculum and beyond. Find out more about Early Years and reading with children from the National Literacy Trust (www.literacytrust.org.uk).

Themed titles
Let's eat Breakfast is one of four **Food We Eat** titles that explore food and meals from around the world. The other titles are:

Let's eat Lunch   **Let's eat Dinner**   **Celebration Food**

Areas of learning
Each **Food We Eat** title helps to support the following Foundation Stage areas of learning:
Personal, Social and Emotional Development
Communication, Language and Literacy
Mathematical Development
Knowledge and Understanding of the World
Creative Development

Reading together
When sharing this book with younger children, take time to explore the pictures together. Encourage children by asking them to find, identify, count or describe different objects. Point out different colours or textures.

Allow quiet spaces in your reading so that children can ask questions or repeat your words. Try pausing mid-sentence so children can predict the next word. This sort of participation develops early reading skills.

Follow the words with your finger as you read them aloud. The main text is in Infant Sassoon, a clear, friendly font specially designed for children learning to read and write. The labels and sound effects on the pages add fun, engage the reader and give children the opportunity to distinguish between different levels of communication. Where appropriate, labels, sound effects or main text may be presented in phonic spelling. Encourage children to imitate the sounds.

As you read the book, you can also take the opportunity to talk about the book itself with appropriate vocabulary, such as "page", "cover", "back", "front", "photograph", "label" and "page number".

You can also extend children's learning by using the books as a springboard for discussion and further activities. There are a few suggestions on the facing page.

Pages 4–5: Breakfast time
Encourage children to keep a food diary, either as a group or individually. Divide a big piece of paper into seven sections, one for each day of the week. Each morning, encourage children to draw, paint or stick photos of what they ate for breakfast.

Pages 6–7: Hot toast
Explain how honey is produced by bees and use as a starting point for role play, with children play-acting being busy bees, collecting nectar and carrying it back to the hive. They can practise special bee dances, to call other bees to a 'flower'.

Pages 8–9: Cereals
Use squares of card to make a simple game of pairs that highlights the provenance of different foodstuffs. Make more than one set of each pair. Pairs could include: oats or corn/field; eggs/chicken; milk/cow; bacon/pig; orange juice/orange tree; cup of tea/tea plant.

Pages 10–11: Pick and mix
Encourage the children to make their own fruit kebabs. Provide cubes of fresh fruit and bamboo skewers, taking care to supervise the use of the skewers.

Pages 12–13: Something to drink
Make-believe a café scenario. Help the children to design simple pictorial menus of breakfast drinks, then role-play being customers or servers. Introduce props such as play-money and a till to enhance the activity with counting.

Pages 14–15: Breakfast eggs
Collect pictures of whole eggs and eggs cooked in different ways and use them to make a poster. Decorate the edge with chicken pictures. This can lead into a discussion of where eggs come from, and which other animals lay eggs.

Pages 16–17: All kinds of bread
Make salt dough and practise kneading it like bread. Shape the salt dough into croissant shapes, and perhaps other pretend breakfast ingredients. Bake, then paint, and use for make-believe breakfast feasts.

Pages 18–19: Rice and fish
A Japanese breakfast includes grilled fish, pickled vegetables, miso (soybean) soup and rice with seaweed. Compile a recipe scrapbook of different breakfasts from around the world. Talk about which breakfast dishes are savoury and which are sweet, which are eaten hot and which cold.

Pages 20–21: Make it: Swiss muesli
Organise a blind tasting of different fresh and dried fruits, including raisins, figs, dried mango, pear and apple. See if children can guess which fruits they are tasting, and rate them according to sweetness, crunchiness, or any other scale they choose.

Index

b
breakfast time **4–5**

c
chapati **16**
cheese **10**
China **18**
congee **18**
croissant **17**

d
drinks **12**

e
eggs **14, 15**

f
fish **19**
fruit **11**

j
Japan **19**

m
meats **10**
milk **13**
muesli **20–21**

o
oats **8, 9**

p
porridge **8, 18**

r
rice **18**

t
toast **6, 7**

Picture acknowledgements:
Alamy: 9 (Stephen Shepherd), 16 (JTB Communications Inc), 17 (Vittore Buzzi);
Corbis: 4–5 (Randy Faris), 13 (Frank Lukasseck/Zefa), 18 (Steve Lupton), 19 (Tibor Bognar); **Evans:** 11 (Gareth Boden); **iStockphoto:** cover tablecloth, 2–3, 6, 12, 22–24 (Jon Helgason), cover sky & wheat (Clint Scholz), cover & 15 (Alan Egginton), 6 (Richard Lloyd), 7 tablecloth (Gaffera), 7tl (Duncan Walker), 7cr (Monika Adamczyk), 7bl (Artem Rebrov), 10 (Rohit Seth), 12tc (Kelly Cline), 12cl (Andrei Nekrassov), 12c (Mikael Damkier), 12cr (Carmen Martínez), 12br (Flavia Bottazzini), 14 (Joe Gough), 22–24 sky (Judy Foldetta); **Photolibrary:** 8 (Joy Skipper), 20–21 (David Marsden).